D1164559

LOOK AT
TEETH AND TUSKS

Franklin Watts Inc.
387 Park Avenue South
New York
N.Y. 10016

US ISBN: 0-531-10723-X
Library of Congress Catalog
Card Number: 89-40011

Design: Edward Kinsey
Illustrations: Simon Roulstone
Phototypeset by Lineage Ltd, Watford
Printed in Italy
by G. Canale & C S.p.A. - Turin

Picture credits:
Animal Photography 21
Bruce Coleman 25
Reg Horlock 4, 5, 26a, 28
Survival Anglia 9, 10, 22
Zefa 6a, 6b, 7a, 7b, 8, 11a, 11b, 12, 13, 14, 15,
16, 17, 18a, 18b, 19, 20, 23, 24, 26a, 26b, 27

LOOK AT
TEETH AND TUSKS

Ruth Thomson

FRANKLIN WATTS
London • New York • Sydney • Toronto

How many teeth do you have ?
You were born with no teeth at all.

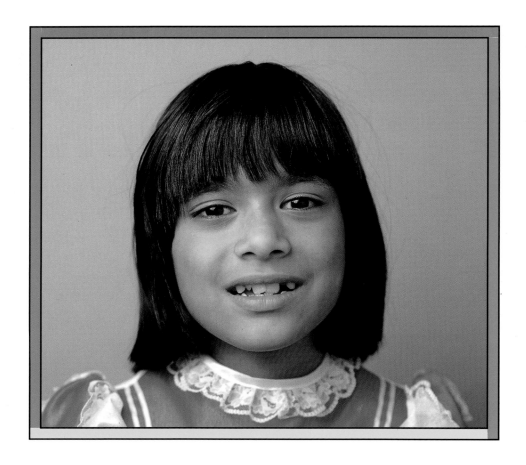

Then your baby teeth grew.
At the age of six, these teeth begin to fall out.
By the time you are an adult you will have
a completely new set of thirty two teeth.

People have biting, gripping and chewing teeth
so they can eat all sorts of food.
Look closely at your teeth in a mirror.
Can you tell what each type of tooth does?

Have you ever looked at the teeth of animals?

Some have particularly big front teeth.

Hamster

Some have a few teeth which are much bigger than their others.

Tiger

Some have broad, blunt teeth.

Sheep

Some have sharp, pointed teeth.

Crocodile

You can often tell what an animal eats by looking at its teeth.

7

Squirrels, mice and hamsters are rodents.
They have strong front teeth, called incisors.
They can bite through very hard things.
A rodent's teeth never stop growing,
but they wear down as the animal feeds.

Beavers have incisors that are so strong they can gnaw through tree trunks.

9

Tusks are really long front teeth.
An elephant uses them to pull bark
off trees or to dig for water.

Walruses use their tusks
to dig for shellfish.

Hippos use their tusks
for fighting.
They use their other teeth
for chewing water plants.

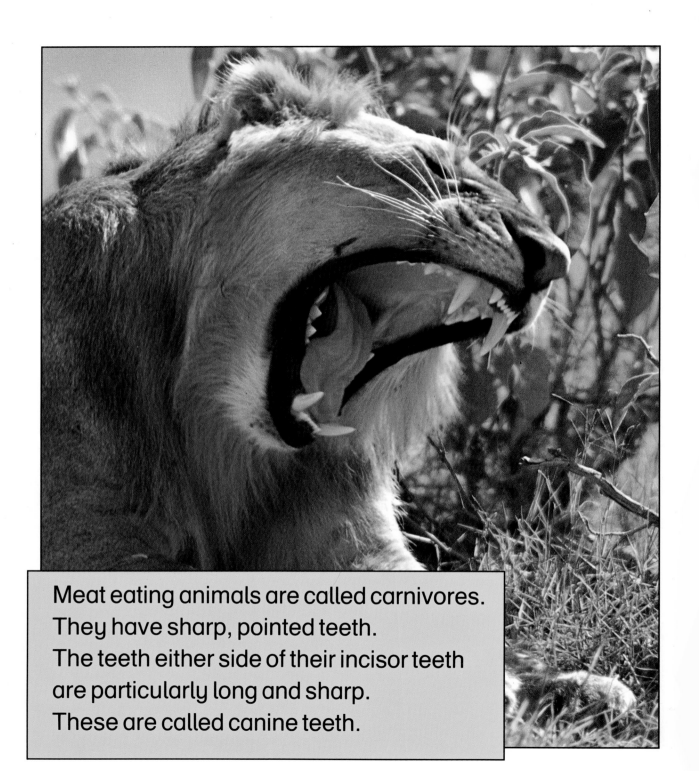

Meat eating animals are called carnivores.
They have sharp, pointed teeth.
The teeth either side of their incisor teeth
are particularly long and sharp.
These are called canine teeth.

Carnivores use their canine teeth
to grip and kill their prey.
They use their other teeth
for chewing the meat.

Plant eaters are called herbivores.
They usually have a big mouth
with long rows of back teeth, called molars.
Molars are wide and blunt.
They are good for chewing and grinding.

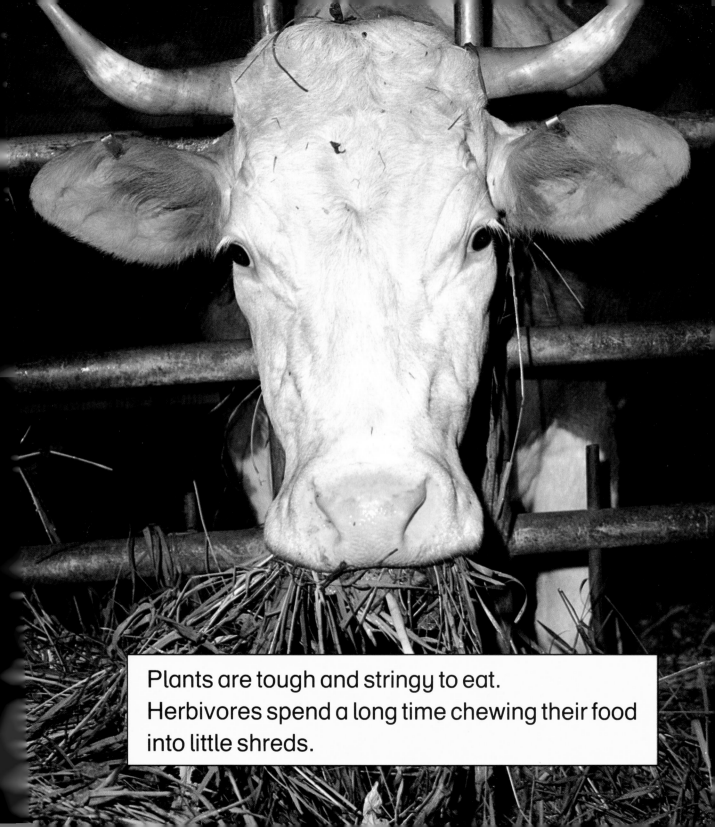

Plants are tough and stringy to eat.
Herbivores spend a long time chewing their food
into little shreds.

Pandas eat bamboo, which is hard and tough.
They have ridged back teeth
that can crunch the bamboo into pieces.

Some goats have no top front teeth.
They have a horny pad instead,
which they use for biting plants.

Animals that catch
and feed on slippery fish
have rows of sharp,
even teeth.

Killer whale

Ghariel

Sharks have several rows of razor sharp teeth. As their front set of teeth wear away, or fall out, new teeth from the row behind replace them.

Some snakes have two long front teeth, called fangs.
Poisonous snakes have hollow fangs.
When a snake bites its prey,
poison is pumped through its fangs into the victim.

The spitting cobra spits poison from its fangs
at its enemy's eyes.
It can spit almost three meters.

Some animals use their teeth
to show their feelings.
Foxes, dogs and wolves bare their teeth
and curl their lip when they are angry.

Many animals have no teeth.
How do they manage to feed?

The frog shoots out
its sticky tongue
to catch insects.

Some animals, like this lizard,
swallow their food whole!

Some whales have a fringe of bony plates
that act like a net.
When the whale opens its mouth,
seawater, with thousands of tiny shrimp, rushes in.
When it closes its mouth, the shrimp stay in
as the water flows out through the bony plates.

Birds have beaks instead of teeth.

The eagle has a hooked beak for tearing flesh.

The woodpecker has a sharp beak for boring into wood.

The curlew has a long, curved beak for finding worms in the mud.

Birds' food is ground in a special stomach,
called a gizzard.
Birds that eat seeds swallow grit,
to help them digest their food.

Often, the food an animal eats helps to keep its teeth clean.

Camel

We have to brush our teeth every day to make sure they stay clean and healthy.

Do you know?

● The shape of an animal's teeth reveals a great deal about its diet.

● We are mammals, who eat a mixed diet. We have biting incisor teeth at the front of our jaws. On either side of the incisors is a single, gripping canine tooth. At the back of our mouth are rows of flatter, chewing teeth, called premolars and molars.

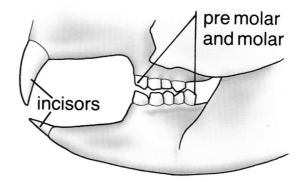

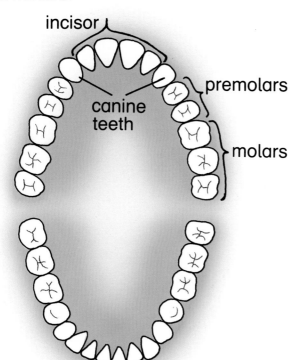

● Mammals that eat mainly insects or fruit have similar kinds of teeth to ours.

● Animals that gnaw their food have no canine teeth at all. Their strong front incisors have hard enamel on only the front surface. The soft dentine on the back wears away as the animal chews, so that the tooth resembles a sharp chisel. This is how rodents can chew through very hard materials, such as metal, glass, wood and concrete.

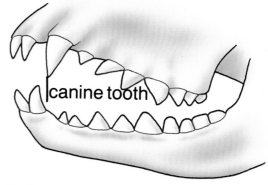

● Carnivores, on the other hand, have tiny incisors, but enormous canine teeth. Their chewing molars are pointed and sharp.

● By contrast the chewing teeth of herbivores are wide and ridged, to grind down plant fibers. Eating tough plants wears down herbivores' teeth. When their teeth wear out, they can no longer feed and so they die.

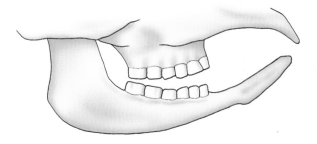

Things to do

● Find out about the eating habits of different animals. Try to answer these questions about each of the animals you choose:

What does it eat — meat, plants or a mixture of both?

When does it eat — for most of the time or only now and again?

How does it use its teeth — to tear, rip, chew or crunch food? Does it use its teeth to pull up food or to dig for it?

What size are its teeth — are they all the same size or are some bigger than others?

Make a chart like the one below to show the relationship between animals' teeth and the kind of food that they eat.

What do you notice?

| | | TYPE OF FOOD | | |
		MEAT OR FISH	PLANT	MIXED
	BIG CANINES	Tiger		
	SAME SIZE SHARP	Killer Whale		
TYPE OF TEETH	BLUNT		Horse	
	STRONG FRONT TEETH		Beaver	

● Some animals do not only use their teeth for eating, they also use them for either fighting or in defense against enemies.

● Collect some pictures of animals using their teeth for attack or defense. Here are some examples to look for:
● The camel stretches its neck and head and gnashes its teeth to threaten rivals.
● The hippo opens its mouth and moves its head round to warn off enemies. It looks as though it is yawning.
● Dogs snarl at one another and bare their canine teeth.
● Elephants use their tusks in fights with each other. Their tusks entangle and the elephants push with all their might until one gives way. Then the winner jabs the side of the loser.

A tooth quiz

● Do some research to find out the answers to these questions:

1. How can you tell the age of a horse by its teeth?

2. How do crocodiles have their teeth cleaned?

3. Which animals have tusks made of ivory? Why can this be a danger to them?

4. Do all mammals have teeth?

Sayings

These are some sayings about animals' teeth. Can you find out what they mean?

To show one's teeth
His bark is worse than his bite
Don't look a gift horse in the mouth.
To hear something straight from the horse's mouth.
To take the bit between one's teeth.
To place oneself in the lion's mouth.

Index

Beaks 26
Beavers 9, 30

Camels 28, 31
Canine Teeth 12, 13, 29, 30
Carnivores (meat eaters) 12,
    13, 29
Crocodile 7, 31
Curlew 26

Dentine 29
Dogs 22, 31

Eagle 26
Elephant 10, 31
Enamel 29

Fangs 20
Foxes 22
Frogs 23

Ghariel 18
Gizzard 27
Goats 17

Hamster 6, 8
Herbivores (plant eaters) 14,
    15, 30
Hippos 11, 31
Horse 14, 30, 31

Incisors 8, 9, 12, 29

Lions 12, 13, 31

Molars 14, 29

Pandas 16
Premolars 29

Rodents 8, 29

Sharks 19
Sheep 7, 31
Shellfish 11, 25
Snakes 20
Squirrel 8

Teeth 4, 5, 6, 7, 8, 11, 12, 13,
    14, 16, 17, 18, 19, 20,
    22, 23, 26, 28, 29, 30, 31
Teeth, care of 28
Tiger 6, 30
Tongue 23
Tusks 10, 11, 31

Walruses 11
Whales 18, 25
Wolves 22